This book was given to me by: _____

My name: _____

My birthday: _____

My address: _____

_____

Here you can put
a photo
of yourself.

I like to: _____

_____

I don't like to: _____

_____

What I really want is: _____

_____

LEARNING
BASKETBALL

Katrin Barth & Lothar Boesing

Sport Science Consultant: Dr. Berndt Barth

Meyer & Meyer Sport

Original title: Ich lerne Basketball
© 2008 by Meyer & Meyer Verlag
Translated by Petra Haynes
AAA Translation, St. Louis, Missouri, USA
www.AAATranslation.com

British Library Cataloguing in Publication Data
A catalogue record for this book is available from the British Library

Learning Basketball
Katrin Barth & Lothar Boesing
Maidenhead: Meyer & Meyer Sport (UK) Ltd., 2009
ISBN: 978-1-84126-250-5

© 2009 by Meyer & Meyer Sport (UK) Ltd.
Aachen, Adelaide, Auckland, Budapest, Cape Town, Graz, Indianapolis,
Maidenhead, New York, Olten (CH), Singapore, Toronto
Member of the World
Sport Publishers' Association (WSPA)
www.w-s-p-a.org
Printed by: B.O.S.S Druck und Medien GmbH
ISBN: 978-1-84126-250-5
E-Mail: verlag@m-m-sports.com
www.m-m-sports.com

.... TABLE OF CONTENTS

Please note:
The exercises and practical suggestions in this book have been carefully
chosen and reviewed by the authors. However, the authors are not liable
for accidents or damages of any kind incurred in connection with the
content of this book.

HI THERE, DEAR BEGINNING BASKETBALL PLAYER! I AM PIT, THE LITTLE PANTHER WITH THE BLUE NOSE.
NO BASKETBALL IS SAFE FROM ME.
IT MAKES TOTAL SENSE, BECAUSE PANTHERS LIKE MYSELF, ARE FAST AND AGILE, SMART AND CUNNING.

IN THIS BOOK YOU WILL LEARN LOTS ABOUT PLAYING BASKETBALL AND I WILL ALWAYS BE THERE WITH YOU. I THINK WE'LL HAVE LOTS OF FUN TOGETHER!

IN THIS BOOK YOU WILL OFTEN SEE SOME PICTURES OF PIT.

Here Pit gives you a tip or some important advice so you can do even better.

Pretty tricky! Sometimes Pit has a task or a puzzler for you. You will find these next to the question mark.

The answers and solutions are in the back of the book.

When you see Pit with a pencil you get to record, fill in or color something.

You can use the basketball book like a diary. Record your progress and your goals. When you have become an experienced player, you can enjoy reading about how it all began. If you like you can add photos of yourself and your team, or collect autographs.

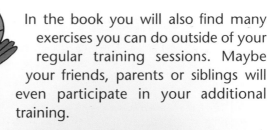

In the book you will also find many exercises you can do outside of your regular training sessions. Maybe your friends, parents or siblings will even participate in your additional training.

In these places you will find a "blank" basketball.

Once you have mastered the technique pretty well or have completed the suggested exercise, you can reward yourself by coloring the basketball with your favorite colors.

If you like you can try it out right now on this first ball!

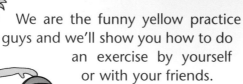

We are the funny yellow practice guys and we'll show you how to do an exercise by yourself or with your friends.

Once you have tried something, color our blank ball.

And I am the little blue mistake guy. I deliberately make mistakes – only to help you, of course! Let's see if you can recognize them all. If you're not sure, check the solution pages.

Pit loves ball games but he can't decide which of the many ball sports to choose. Which ball sports do you recognize in this picture?

Do you know any more ball sports? List them here!

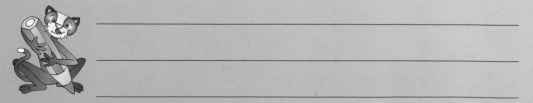

_____

_____

_____

........1 DEAR BEGINNING BASKETBALL PLAYER

You are probably one of those ball-crazy kids who can't come across a ball without wanting to play with it. There's an itch in your hands and you immediately want to chase after the ball, catch it, dribble it and throw it. Sometimes it is a cute little bouncy ball, a brightly colored rubber ball or a tennis ball. It's just plain fun!

But it's even more fun when there are other children around and you can play ball with each other, make up games and rules and compete against each other.

Is that how you became interested in basketball? Or was it your friends, your parents or your siblings, who gave you basketball fever and got you excited? Do they already play for a club? Or maybe you got the idea to learn to play basketball from those cool street players, from watching basketball games on television or seeing the stars of the NBA.

In any case, you have chosen a great sport that is very popular all around the world.

11

Here are a few reasons why children like to play basketball. Which ones apply to you? Check "yes" or "no"!

	YES	NO
I enjoy running around and playing sports.	☐	☐
I like being with other children.	☐	☐
I want to play on a team.	☐	☐
I am already very involved in sports.	☐	☐
I am tall and therefore probably well suited.	☐	☐
I am nimble and have a good feel for the ball.	☐	☐
I am assertive.	☐	☐
I like watching ball games.	☐	☐
My friends can also play basketball.	☐	☐
I want to be better than others.	☐	☐
I want to rank among the best in my country.	☐	☐
I want to become a pro and be really famous.	☐	☐

If you answered most of these questions with "yes," you have chosen the right sport!

Many girls and boys learn to play basketball in a club. They practice regularly, play on teams and compete against other teams. But you don't have to be a member of a club to play basketball. A ball, a basket, and an open space, add a few friends – you're ready to play!

In this basketball book we have listed many interesting things about your favorite sport. We explain the most important techniques, how to practice them and which mistakes to avoid. You will receive numerous suggestions for practicing alone or with friends.

There are also many game ideas to try out. Of course Mom, Dad, your grandparents, siblings and anyone who – like you – enjoys it, is invited to practice.

The players got permission to decorate a wall in their locker room with graffiti. Use a fun color to fill in all the fields that have a dot!

Can you tell what it says?

Some day you may be a super-successful player at the national level or the top player on a successful team. But even if for you basketball remains a recreational sport, you will notice how much you enjoy this sport.

You learn to play together with others, to become part of a team and to assert yourself. You make new friends, meet many interesting people and are part of the large "basketball family." You learn to fight and have willpower. You won't always be the glorious winner. You will also learn to deal with defeat, botched shots on basket, bad passes or poor receiving. And soon you will notice that playing basketball regularly is giving you more endurance, making you faster and stronger, and keeping your body fit and healthy.

This little book is intended to be your companion as you learn to play basketball. If we ever view something differently from the way your coach, trainer or an experienced player explains it – that can sometimes happen. Then just ask questions. Even in basketball opinions sometimes differ.

When we refer to trainers, coaches, players, referees, etc., we of course are not just talking about men and boys, but also about women and girls.

Have fun playing basketball!
The authors and
the little panther, Pit.

15

HAVE YOU HAD A LAUGH TODAY?

THE ELEPHANT AND THE MOUSE ARE PLAYING BASKETBALL. THE ELEPHANT ACCIDENTALLY STEPS ON THE MOUSE'S FOOT. "OH, I AM SO SORRY," SAYS THE ELEPHANT. "NO BIG DEAL," SAYS THE MOUSE. "THAT COULD HAVE HAPPENED TO ME, TOO!"

THE ELEPHANT AND THE MOUSE WANT TO PRACTICE ARITHMETIC. THE ELEPHANT ASKS: "WHAT'S 75 AND 75?" ANSWERS THE MOUSE: "THAT'S EASY. IT'S A TIE!"

THE MOUSE IS SITTING IN THE STANDS WATCHING A BASKETBALL GAME. SUDDENLY THE ELEPHANT ARRIVES AND SITS DOWN RIGHT IN FRONT OF HER. THE MOUSE SQUEAKS: "I CAN'T SEE!" NO REACTION FROM THE ELEPHANT. THE MOUSE SQUEAKS AGAIN: "I CAN'T SEE!" STILL NO REACTION FROM THE ELEPHANT. THE ANGRY MOUSE MOVES TO A SEAT RIGHT IN FRONT OF THE ELEPHANT. SAYS THE MOUSE: "MAYBE NOW YOU CAN SEE WHAT IT'S LIKE WHEN SOMEONE SITS RIGHT IN FRONT OF YOU!"

THE ELEPHANT IS SWIMMING HAPPILY IN THE LAKE. THE MOUSE WALKS UP AND SAYS: "QUICK, GET OUT OF THE WATER!" THE ELEPHANT DOESN'T WANT TO GET OUT AND KEEPS SWIMMING. AGAIN THE MOUSE SAYS EXCITEDLY: "PLEASE GET OUT! IT'S REALLY IMPORTANT!" THE ELEPHANT GETS OUT OF THE WATER AND THE MOUSE SAYS: "OK, YOU CAN GET BACK IN. I JUST WANTED TO MAKE SURE YOU ARE WEARING SWIMMING TRUNKS."

. . . . 2 HOW BASKETBALL BEGAN

The ball certainly has always been people's favorite piece of sports and play equipment. But no one really knows how ball games actually began. But it was definitely so long ago that there were no videotapes, no photos, not even books. But researchers discovered ancient cave drawings depicting people playing with something ball-like.

Basketball is the most widespread team sport in the world. Many people love this fast and exciting game; they play themselves or watch the games with fascination. Just like you! Many basketball players are stars like pop-singers or actors.

You may think that basketball originated in the United States, but that's not quite right. The idea of throwing a ball through a hoop is much, much older. You can see on the following pages how this sport evolved.

The origin

As early as 3000 years ago, people in Central and South America played games where a ball had to be thrown through hoops. They were the Inca, Maya and Aztecs. But other people also always enjoyed throwing balls or taking shots at a target.

Ball games evolved

Different ball games evolved from just having fun playing with a ball and a target. So today we have handball, volleyball, soccer, hockey, etc.

Basketball's anniversary

More than one hundred years ago, there was an American college professor from Springfield, Massachusetts, by the name of James Nalsmith. He played baseball and football with his students at the YMCA training school and wanted to come up with an indoor game for those cold winter days.
This new game should be fun for everyone and shouldn't be as rough as football. Because football is such a physical game, too many students were getting injured each year.

The professor nailed two fruit baskets to the walls on the narrow sides of the gymnasium, formed two teams and handed them a ball. They were ready to play! Of course the players were always excited about making a basket. But in the beginning there was one little problem: the ball would be in the basket and the janitor had to get it down.

Olympic basketball

An exhibition basketball tournament was held as early as 1904, at the St. Louis Olympics. But not until 1930, did the International Olympic Committee (IOC) decide to add basketball to the tournament schedule of the Olympics.

Variations

Basketball continues to evolve. The rules are adjusted and the manufacturers of sporting goods do research on improved materials for balls, baskets and court surfaces. There also continue to be new clothing trends.

STREET BALL

Street basketball is a good opportunity to also play outside, away from the gym. Friends meet with a ball at an outdoor court and the game is on. But there are also organized street ball tournaments with set rules.

BEACH BASKETBALL

Sunshine, sand and beach atmosphere – that's fun! Beach basketball is one of the new fun sports. Of course the techniques have to be adjusted because dribbling on the sand hardly works, but at least the ground is softer when a player falls.

WHEELCHAIR BASKETBALL

Wheelchair basketball is very popular with disabled athletes nationally and internationally. The rules are pretty similar. This also allows disabled and able-bodied players to play together. Of course every player sits in a wheelchair.

BASKETBALL IS A TEAM SPORT

Like many other sports, basketball also is a team sport. That's what's so special and nice about this sport. The athlete doesn't compete alone but is part of a team. Everyone does his best for the mutual victory.

It is important that the athletes are able to train and play together regularly. That is why permanent teams are formed in clubs. Teams in various age groups play in tournaments and have rankings.

What is the name of your club?

_____

Which team are you on?

_____

You can paste or draw your club's logo here.

NATIONAL ASSOCIATIONS

Write down the name of the national basketball association in your country:

_____

Put the logo of your basketball association here:

BASKETBALL IN THE UNITED STATES – NBA

There are three major basketball associations in the United States:

• The United States Basketball Association for youth basketball.
• The National Collegiate Basketball Association for college players, founded in 1905.
• The National Basketball Association for professional basketball, founded in 1949.

If you would you like to learn more about the history or get some current information, check out the Internet at:
www.usbahoops.com, www.ncaa.com, www.nba.com

21

U.S. BASKETBALL CHAMPIONSHIPS

The men's teams and the women's teams compete in their own respective championship series. The champions are determined at the end of the season.

Year	Men's champions

Year	Women's champions

Here you can keep a list of champions. Record the most recent stats. Write the year in the left column and the team in the right column. Start with the current year.

PICTOGRAMS

Surely you have seen different sports depicted as drawings or symbols on television, in the newspaper, on stickers or posters. These symbols are called pictograms. The drawing is very simple, yet everyone immediately recognizes the correct sport.

Here you can see such a pictogram for basketball.

How would you illustrate basketball using very simple lines? Here is a place for your ideas!

. . . . 3 HI THERE, DIRK!

Dirk Nowitzki
Born June 19, 1978 in Würzburg, Germany
Height: 6'9"
Weight: 245 lbs.
Successful player on the German national team
Currently ranked best European player in the NBA

Hi there, Dirk! How did you get involved in basketball?

Even as a little boy I always enjoyed contact with the ball. Playing with my friends also was important to me. Because I grew very quickly I did very well in basketball at school.

What do you think is so great about this sport?

You have to be quick but must be able to throw accurately. The rules promote playing fairly with each other.

How did you manage to become so successful? What's your secret?

There is no secret. You constantly have to work on yourself and try to get better.

What abilities must a good basketball player have?

You need the willingness to always continue to work on yourself, to improve your technique and your fitness level. And you have to enjoy being a team player.

Which was your greatest or your most important success?

Taking third place at the 2002 World Championships in Indianapolis and also second place with the German national team at the 2005 European Championships were great successes.

What are your goals?

Participating in the Olympics would be nice. Aside from that I would like to still try to win the NBA championship.

How often do you practice?

Before the start of the season I practice several times a day. During the season practices are once a day.

Do you sometimes not feel like practicing? What do you do?

That's not so unusual. But then I just have to push past it and go to practice anyway. That's when I do mostly technical exercises: very carefully, slowly, but as perfect as possible.

Are you interested in any other sports? What hobbies do you have?

Reading and good music are awesome. I also like to watch tennis and soccer.

You are a role model for many children and adolescents. Do you have a tip for these boys and girls?

Always have fun with our great game. Never get discouraged and continue to try to get better.

THANK YOU VERY MUCH FOR THE INTERVIEW AND LOTS OF LUCK IN THE FUTURE!

FAN PAGE

My favorite male or female player:

_____

Team:

_____

Photo

My favorite team:

_____

_____

_____

Logo

_____

Here you can collect autographs from players or paste photos.

Here is a place for photos of you or your team.

. . . . . . 4 NO PAIN, NO GAIN

Surely you have dreamt about what it would be like to be the best. Everyone cheers you on, is in awe and admires you. The most successful teams want you to join. The fans assail you and want your autograph.

You are deadly at the basket and tops in defense. Almost every opponent loses to you when playing one-on-one; your dribbling and passing technique and your shots on the basket are amazing. For that you accept congratulations from your teammates, your coach, your fans, your friends and parents …!

But stop! Just lying in the grass dreaming of success isn't enough!

If you want to be a good basketball player, maybe even better than the others, you have to practice often and diligently. That's not always easy and isn't always fun right away.

Diligence precedes success!

GOALS

When you begin to play basketball you need to answer the following questions:

 What is my goal?

 With what can I reach my goal?

 How can I reach my goal?

 What is my goal? Why do I practice so much?

Just playing the ball back and forth is fun. But soon you'll likely wish you could catch the ball more reliably and quickly, pass more accurately and especially score. Your friends should pick you for their team because you are a reliable player and really support the others. Maybe you would like to finally play on a school team or start on a higher division team. What would it be like to be discovered by a scout for the NBA and play for a top team?

Of course you are still too young for that. Nevertheless, you should already have bigger goals today. You have to know what you want. If you don't have a goal, practicing soon won't be fun anymore. So you continue to set higher goals for yourself. That's what the successful players have done.

Why do you want to learn to play basketball?
List your goals here!

_____

_____

_____

With what can I reach my goal?

Of course now you will want to know what you can do to improve your performance. Definitely play lots and lots of basketball! Add to that the necessary exercises to get the feel for the ball, technique training, as well as endurance and strength training, which the basketball coach will do with you. There will definitely be some things you won't enjoy very much. Some things may seem boring and much too strenuous. But all of these exercises will help you reach your goal.

How can I reach my goal?

How are things going now that you continue to improve with regular practice? As long as the exercises are easy and relaxed the muscles will only do what they already know. Only when something is strenuous and the movements are no longer so easy, are the muscles getting stronger. So you have to work hard and put some strain on your body to make progress.

When you haven't been to basketball practice for a while you will notice that you have gotten a little worse and are a little winded. Now you have to catch up!

The more diligently and frequently you practice, the better you will be!

33

PHYSICAL FITNESS IS IMPORTANT

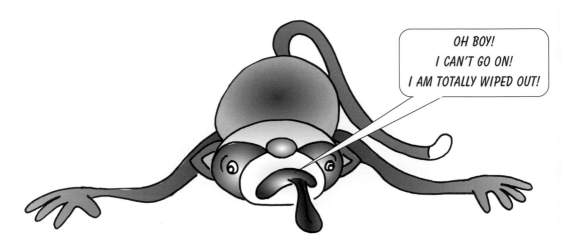

**OH BOY!
I CAN'T GO ON!
I AM TOTALLY WIPED OUT!**

Oh dear! What's wrong with Pit? After playing basketball for only ten minutes he is so exhausted that he can barely stand up.

Has that ever happened to you? Do you also get winded so easily and lose your strength quickly? Then you need to work on your fitness level!

What should a good basketball player be able to do? Cross out the things that are not as important. If we forgot anything, write it down!

Ski   Run fast   Play the flute

Handle the ball   Jump   Dribble
skillfully   Change direction quickly

Watch closely   Exercise for   Throw accurately
an hour

Change running speed   Tell jokes

What is physical fitness?

When playing basketball you have to run a lot, handle the ball skillfully, take powerful jumps, throw accurately and always be alert. Can you do that for an extended period of time? Then you are probably pretty fit. If not, the game soon won't be as fun and you should work on improving your fitness level. You do that primarily by practicing regularly.

What do you need?

You need **endurance** to handle physical exertion for an extended period of time. Then you won't get winded so fast when running, jumping, bicycling or swimming. When it does get strenuous, you will recover quickly and feel fit again.

If you want to be able to run, jump, start really fast and still be able to always keep your balance, you need strong leg muscles. **Strength** in your arms, hands and fingers is also important so you can grip the ball, throw it accurately and catch it well.

For a basketball player it is also important to be able to cover the court quickly and react instantly. For that you need **speed**.

Sometimes you jump really high, throw from a difficult position or catch a poorly thrown pass. Good **flexibility** is also important if you want to skillfully dribble around the opponent.

At practice you won't just run the ball down the court to the basket. Surely your coach will have you play other ball games, as well as exercises and calisthenics. Really participate because all of these things will help improve your physical fitness level.

THIS IS HOW YOU CAN PRACTICE

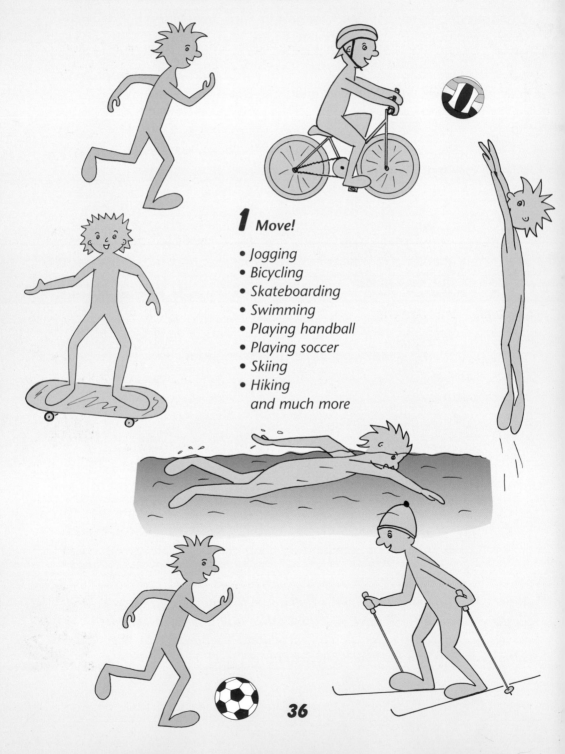

1 Move!

- *Jogging*
- *Bicycling*
- *Skateboarding*
- *Swimming*
- *Playing handball*
- *Playing soccer*
- *Skiing*
- *Hiking*
  and much more

36

2 *Fast and agile*

• Slalom run
Set up a slalom course using poles, cones or other objects. Run through it without making mistakes and keep trying to lower your time.

• High and low
Set up a course with several low hurdles in a row. The runner jumps over the first hurdle, crawls under the next hurdle, jumps over the next one again, etc.

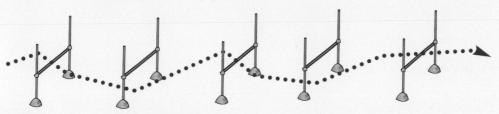

3 *Balance and dexterity*

• Keeping your balance
Try balancing on one leg for an extended period of time. As you do so, sing a song, clap your hands, make faces or silly movements.

• Balancing
Balance your way along a chalk line or a beam. You maybe able to find some low walls in your neighborhood or some logs in the woods to balance on.

• Dexterity exercises
Many athletic exercises require dexterity and skill. Try inline skating, ice skating, walking on stilts, riding a mountain bike or a unicycle. Have you ever juggled?

Which sport other than basketball do you enjoy?

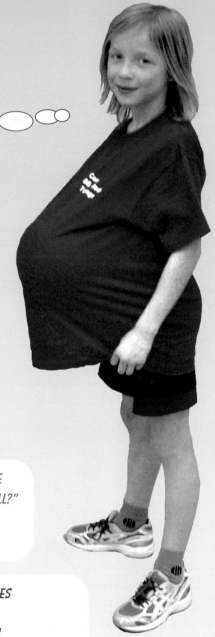

I REALLY DON'T KNOW
WHERE THE BALL IS.
HAVE YOU SEEN IT?

THE COACH ASKS MAX:
"WHY DO YOU COME TO PRACTICE WITH
THOSE DIRTY HANDS?"
ANSWERS MAX:
"I DON'T HAVE ANY OTHER ONES!"

TINA WATCHES PAUL PLAY BASKETBALL. FINALLY SHE
ASKS HIM: "DO YOU REALLY ENJOY PLAYING BASKETBALL?"
"OF COURSE!" SAYS MAX.
"THEN WHY DON'T YOU LEARN TO PLAY?"

THE BASKETBALL COACH APPROACHES
THE TELEVISION COMMENTATOR:
"PLEASE SPEAK A LITTLE SLOWER!
MY PLAYERS CAN'T RUN AS FAST AS YOU TALK!"

. . . . 5 BASKETBALL EQUIPMENT

Even a beginning basketball player wants to look like a real basketball player.

BUT WHAT DOES THAT TAKE?

You can play basketball in any type of sportswear. That includes a pair of pants, a shirt, socks and tennis shoes. Everything should be comfortable and not interfere with your playing. On the court the right shoes with non-skid soles are especially important. They should provide good support when you run and jump.

Of course it would be great if at some point you got a real basketball jersey, matching socks and awesome shoes. But in the beginning that's not really necessary.

When you play for a club the teams are given matching uniforms for their games.

THE CLOTHES

For basketball practice you wear casual clothes that are comfortable and practical.

That includes:

Pants and shirt

Pants and shirt should be comfortable and not hinder your movements.

Practice games

During practices teams are always formed. To be able to distinguish who plays on which team the players on each team wear shirts of the same color.

Shoes

The shoes must fit well and provide good support during sprints, when changing direction and jumping.

Light-colored or skid-proof soles prevent ugly skid marks on the court.

THE COURT

A good place for playing basketball – be it with one or more people – can easily be found.

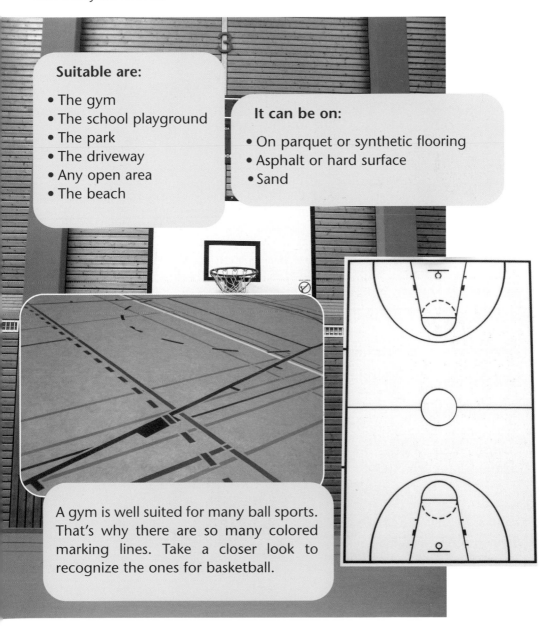

Suitable are:

- The gym
- The school playground
- The park
- The driveway
- Any open area
- The beach

It can be on:

- On parquet or synthetic flooring
- Asphalt or hard surface
- Sand

A gym is well suited for many ball sports. That's why there are so many colored marking lines. Take a closer look to recognize the ones for basketball.

THE BALL

A basketball player needs a basketball. What would basketball be without a ball?

Balls are available from different manufacturers in various sizes and colors. They are made from synthetic materials or leather – cheap and really expensive.

A size 5 ball would be right for you. Make sure it is inflated properly. (If you drop the ball from a height of six feet it should bounce back up at least four feet.)

If there isn't a basketball available for you to practice dribbling, passing, catching and shooting, then find another ball. Playing with different balls is fun and improves the feel for the ball.

The rules dictate that special balls must be used for tournaments. The **tournament ball** has a leather or synthetic shell that is filled with air. They come in different sizes for different age groups.

THE BASKET

Sometimes you may play one-on-one with just one basket, with two teams and one basket or, like a real basketball game, with two teams and two baskets.

Almost every gym has **basketball hoops**. Most of the time they are attached to the walls.

Sturdy hoop systems made of metal are appropriate for parks and public courts.

Mobile hoop systems can be set up wherever people want to play basketball. Conveniently, the height of the basket is adjustable.

If possible have a basketball hoop put up in your **driveway**, **backyard** or the **common area of your neighborhood**. A hoop with adjustable height would be best.

No access to a basketball hoop? Then set up a wastebasket or a pail. That's guaranteed to be a lot of fun, too.

These are the things that go in your gym bag. Did we forget anything? Draw it or write it down!

Fruit for
a snack.

Water or water
and juice mix
for when you
are thirsty.

Toiletries for
showering.

A hat is important
on cold days after
sweating and
showering.

Your lucky charm.

Just a few sweets
can sometimes
be important.

Basketball players need warm
muscles. That's why they wear
warm-ups before the game and
during breaks to keep from
getting chilled.

EVERYTHING PACKED?

You are very excited because you are going to an out-of-town game. You practiced lots and the team lineup is set. But imagine you arrive at the game location, unpack your gym bag and... where are the shoes? Your well-broken in awesome playing shoes are at home – far away! Just plain forgotten! There is no one to borrow shoes from, and they wouldn't fit you properly anyway. The fact that you can't play now is not only irritating to you, but it is also a big problem for your team.

Your parents could of course help pack your bag, but every player is responsible for his own complete and clean equipment!

THE CHECKLIST

Many athletes know that anxious feeling of forgetting something for an important game or tournament. That is why it is important to prepare everything ahead of time. Pack your gym bag the night before so you can go to bed with your mind at ease.

Many athletes have found the checklist to be useful. You write down everything you want to bring along. Anything that's packed is checked off. Use a pencil so you can erase the checks for the next time you pack.

MY CHECKLIST

- ☐ JERSEY
- ☐ SHORTS
- ☐ SOCKS
- ☐ SHOES
- ☐ WARM-UPS
- ☐ SHOWER ITEMS
- ☐ _____
- ☐ _____
- ☐ _____
- ☐ _____
- ☐ _____

Use the blank lines to write down anything else you can't forget.

.... 6 A FEEL FOR THE BALL

WHAT EXACTLY IS A FEEL FOR THE BALL?

Is it the happiness the ball feels when it goes in the basket?

OH YEAH!

Or is it the pain it feels when it bounces really hard?

OUCH, OUCH!

OH, MY DEAR, DEAR BALL!
I LOVE YOU SO MUCH!
I'M SORRY THAT I HAVE TO BE
SO ROUGH WITH YOU ALL THE TIME!

Or is it about the feelings the basketball player has for the ball?

THIS IS A FEEL FOR THE BALL

A feel for the ball refers to how well a player can sense the ball with his hand. He feels the ball with his hand; senses how much strength he needs to hold, dribble and pass the ball, or how much force is required for a shot on the basket. How heavy is the ball, how easily does it slip from my hand and how can I hold on to it?

Ten players and one ball! Whoever handles the ball best on the court will win! During a game you want to be able to control the ball.

You receive your teammate's pass and swiftly pass it on. Then you dribble around the opponent or take the ball away from him and make a direct shot into the basket. You're the boss and you show the ball what's what! Not the other way around.

At the same time you have to react quickly. In basketball the player is not allowed to catch the ball, hold on to it and then think about how to proceed. He must make quick decisions and react fast as lightning. That can only be done with a good feel for the ball. It has to almost become an extension of your body. You acquire this feel for the ball with lots and lots of practice.

Even the best basketball players continue to do exercises with the ball. It would be best if you made a little time for that every day. You will find exercises on the following pages.

Have fun!

CULTIVATING THE FEEL FOR THE BALL

Where can you practice?

You don't need much space for the exercises. You can practice in front of your house, in the backyard, at the park, and even inside if it doesn't disturb anyone. But you have to be careful that nothing gets broken.

What can you practice with?

The basketball is your instrument. You should practice with it most of the time. But you can also try out different balls and practice with, for instance, a tennis ball or a small rubber ball.

How can you practice?

You can practice standing up, sitting down on the floor or in a chair. Pick up a ball and just play with it. You can throw it in the air, catch it or dribble it.

A player should of course be able to handle the ball very nimbly. But that doesn't happen right away. You initially do the exercises slowly and then try to get faster each time.

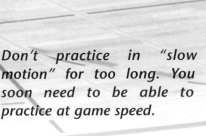

Don't practice in "slow motion" for too long. You soon need to be able to practice at game speed.

THE PERFECT WAY TO HOLD THE BALL

The basketball is held in a way that allows the player to instantly dribble, pass or take a shot at the basket.

This is what you have to pay attention to:

• The ball is held with your fingers loosely spread apart.
• The palms do not touch the ball.
• The fingers are firmly on the ball.
• The wrists are tilted back slightly.

There is a gap between palms and ball.

The thumbs are pointing in direction of the body and are positioned close together.

50

We heard a story about a coach who did an experiment with his players. A basketball was covered in black paint and the players had to play with it. After the game all of the players showed their hands.

Of course the blackened ball really rubbed off onto the players' hands. But where was the black paint visible? Draw it in here!

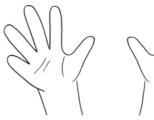

THIS IS HOW YOU CAN PRACTICE THE FEEL FOR THE BALL

Someone who has a good feel for the ball and can skillfully catch, throw and dribble can assure his team's possession of the ball. If you are uncertain when handling the ball, the opponent can quickly take it away from you. That means practice, practice, practice!

1 Throwing it up in the air and catching it

Throw the ball up in the air while standing and catch it with both hands.

- *Turn halfway around / all the way around before you catch it.*
- *Clap your hands in front / behind your back before you catch it.*
- *Vary the height of your throws (low/high).*
- *Catch the ball behind your back.*

2 Rolling the ball forward and back

Roll the ball forward and back alongside your body. Alternately roll it with the right hand and the left hand.

3 Rolling the ball around your body

Roll the ball alongside your body. While doing so the ball always has contact with your body.

- *Roll the ball while standing.*
- *Roll the ball while sitting.*
- *Roll the ball while kneeling.*
- *Roll the ball while lying down.*

4 Rolling a figure eight

You stand with your legs in a slight straddle and roll the ball around your feet in a figure eight. Use the right hand to roll around your right foot and the left hand to roll around your left foot.

• Try looking at the ball less and less often.
• Start out slow and keep increasing your speed.

5 Juggling the ball

• Hold the ball in your open palm while walking around a marker and back again. Turn it into a competition. Who is fastest?
  • Can you do it with only the left or right hand?
  • Dribble the ball from hand to hand.

6 Circling the ball

Guide the ball around your body.

• The ball can be rolled along the stomach and the back.
• The ball can only be passed from one hand to the other without touching the body.
• Circle the ball around to the right and then to the left.

7 Dribbling

Dribble the ball with the right hand/ the left hand.

  • Vary the dribbling height.
  • Dribble the ball from the right hand to the left and back (in front / behind your body).
  • Dribble the ball all the way around your body.

Once you have tried an exercise and practiced it a few times you can color in the corresponding ball.

Just record how many times a week you practice.

Write down the week in the top row and then draw a line underneath every time you practiced.

WEEK	1.	2.						
NUMBER	////-/							

.............7 DRIBBLING, PASSING, CATCHING, SHOOTING BASKETS

What could be more exciting in basketball than burying the ball in the basket or getting a teammate open for a shot on the basket! Sometimes you take a long shot or succeed in making a spectacular lay-up. You skillfully outplay, deke and out-dribble your opponents. The spectators are thrilled.

Maybe you also drive the opposing team near to despair when you win every one-on-one, intercept the hardest ball, make expert passes and pass the ball to your teammate with millimeter accuracy.

All of these successful actions are the result of diligent practice. For every game situation there are special techniques that need to be practiced again and again. Therefore it is important that you know exactly how each move progresses.

On the following pages we show the most important moves for the beginning basketball player.

Which player is passing the ball to his teammate?

WHAT A GOOD BASKETBALL PLAYER MUST HAVE

In order for the game to be fun, even a beginning basketball player must learn important techniques, be able to apply them correctly and master simple game situations.

That includes:

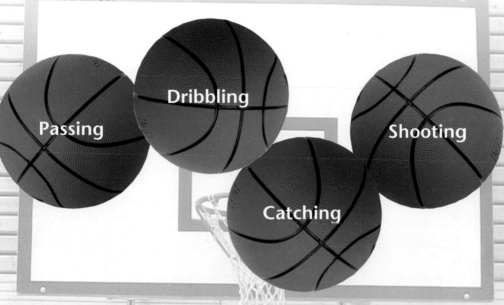

In this book we describe the basic techniques for that. We show you what the technique looks like, what you must pay attention to, how you can practice and which mistakes can crop up during the proper execution.

The best way to learn is to have your coach or an experienced player show you what the technique looks like and then practice it as a group. Back at home you can take your time reviewing the pictures and descriptions in the book.

But now it's time to practice, practice, practice!

THE BASIC POSITION

Basketball is a fast game. All the players must be very alert and follow the game situation. Will someone pass to me or do I have to make a fast catch and then start quickly? Do I have to dodge the opponent and pass to a teammate? A basketball player wants to react as fast as lightning.

That is why a basketball player is always in "starting position" - even when he doesn't have the ball. Basketball players refer to it as the basic position. All joints are flexed and ready for any move. This basic position is the starting position for most techniques in basketball.

This is what you have to pay attention to:

 You pay close attention to the action.

That way you are always ready to receive the ball and don't miss any opportunities.

 Your shoulders are rotated forward slightly, your torso is erect and your eyes are focused on the target.

That allows your body to already face the ball and will make it easier to catch a pass and play it on.

 The arms are slightly bent alongside the body, the wrists are tilted back a little and the fingers spread.

This allows you to quickly catch the ball, pass it, dribble it or shoot it.

 Your feet are shoulder-width apart in a parallel position and the knees and hips are slightly flexed. Your weight is distributed evenly between both feet.

That gives you a firm stance but you are able to quickly run in any direction.

Of course there aren't any fast rules about how much you have to flex your joints or how high the arms and hands should be. Figure out on your own which position is best for you!

The shoulders are rotated forward slightly and the back is rounded just a little.

You pay close attention to the game.

All joints are slightly flexed: ankles, knees, hips.

The legs are in a slight straddle.

59

GOOD OR NOT GOOD?

Take a look at how the players are standing during the game.
Which posture do you think is good and which isn't so good?

You will find the answers in the solutions chapter.

DRIBBLING

People watching a basketball game are always thrilled by the players' dribbling skills. Although many players enjoy dribbling, it is not for entertainment but an important technique in basketball.

Basketball rules do not allow you to run down the court with the ball in your hand. But you are allowed to move while dribbling the ball. Doing so you can dodge your opponents, get yourself in a good passing position or move closer to the basket.

You can dribble with the right or left hand. If possible, try to dribble on the side of your body that is farthest from the opponent. That allows you to also use your body to protect the ball from the defender.

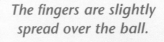

The fingers are slightly spread over the ball.

The eyes are directed forward, away from the ball.

The right or left hand dribbles the ball alongside and slightly in front of the body.

How high you dribble depends on how far away your opponent is.

This is how you dribble

When dribbling the ball is continuously pushed against the floor without holding on to it or even catching it in between. But you can alternate hands.

- The ball is dribbled with the fingers slightly spread apart. Don't "slap" the ball with your open palm. (You should barely hear anything).

- The ball is pushed with a downward motion that originates in the wrist and elbow joints.

- You dribble the ball so hard that it bounces back up to your hand.

- The forearm gives as you "suck up" the ball.

- The ball is carried at elbow level.

If the opponent is far away you can dribble the ball high with an erect posture.

If the opponent is close, lower your torso and dribble very low. You will be better able to protect the ball this way.

ATTENTION – OBSERVE THE RULES!

Dribbling allows you to move the ball very quickly down the court and in doing so get yourself into a good passing or shooting position. You will hugely impress the opponents and the spectators with this.

But if you make a mistake while dribbling you will disadvantage your team because they will lose possession of the ball. That is why you need to know the most important rules and practice lots and lots!

Dribbling can only be successful if you don't break the rules.

This is what you have to pay attention to:

- If you start out dribbling, the ball must touch the floor simultaneously with your first step.

- The ball must always stay below the dribbling hand. (Don't carry the ball!)

- Once you have stopped dribbling and picked up the ball you cannot resume dribbling. You have to pass or take a shot on the basket. You can protect the ball from your opponents by doing a pivot step.

- You can dribble with the right or the left hand as well as alternate hands. There's just one thing you can't do: dribble the ball with both hands at the same time.

When you dribble you have to pay attention to your teammates, your opponent and the game situation. There is no time to review the rules. With lots of practice you will eventually get it right automatically.

MISTAKES YOU SHOULD AVOID WHEN DRIBBLING

Take a look at the players' posture as they dribble. What are they doing wrong?

1

2

Skillful dribbling assures ball possession!

THIS IS HOW YOU CAN PRACTICE DRIBBLING

Someone with a good feel for the ball, who can skillfully dribble, assures his team possession of the ball. If you are not steady when dribbling the opponent can quickly take the ball away from you. That means practice, practice, practice!

1 Dribbling standing up

You can dribble standing up, sitting down or kneeling, with the right hand or the left.

- *Hit the ball, making only brief contact with the ball.*
- *Dribble the ball and make your contact with the ball as long as possible.*
- *Dribble the ball at your side forward and back.*
- *While dribbling, switch from the right to the left hand.*

2 Dribbling a figure eight

You stand in a slight straddle and dribble the ball around your feet in a figure eight. Dribble with your right hand around your right foot and with your left hand around your left foot.

- *While looking at the ball and not looking at the ball.*
- *First slowly and then increasingly faster.*
- *Continue dribbling the course even as someone tries to interfere.*

3 Dribbling while running

- Dribble the ball in a straight line. Alternately go slower and faster and even build in some turns.

  - Choose a marking line on the floor or draw a line on the pavement with chalk and then try to dribble only on the line.

- You have an advantage over your opponent if you can quickly switch hands and continue dribbling. So practice with your right hand and your left and alternate between the two.

4 Dribbling a course

Set up a course of straight-aways, slalom and curves.

- Dribble the course without any mistakes.
- Dribble the course as fast as you can.
- Dribble the course even as someone tries to interfere.

5 Dribbling and passing

The most important thing after you dribble is of course the pass to the teammate or a shot at the basket. Therefore you should always practice that combination.

- Dribble up to a marker, stop, and from there take a shot at the basket.
- Dribble in a straight line up to a marker, stop, and from there dribble in a different direction.
- Mark a target that you would like to hit with a pass after dribbling.

STOPPING

You dribble quickly down the court to get in a good position for a pass or a shot on the basket. To make an accurate pass to your teammate or a successful shot at the basket you have to stop and take hold of the ball.

Jump stop

This type of stop is also called single-leg stop-jump. You jump off with your right or left foot and land on both feet. With this stop you have a choice of the supporting leg for the pivot step. This is how you come to a stop:

• *From a run you jump off with the left or right leg.*

• *You hold the ball with both hands.*

• *You land on both feet.*

Stop!

When you stop you have to be very careful not to make the mistake of traveling with the ball.

When you land your feet are about shoulder-width apart and your knees are slightly bent.

Your torso remains erect!

One-two step stop

This stop is also called double-leg jump. You jump off with one foot, land on the other foot, and the leg you jumped off with swings forward and brings you to a stop. The feet land slightly staggered in a stride position:

• *From a run you jump off with the left foot.*

    • *You land on the right foot.*

        • *Your left leg swings forward and stops your momentum.*

Stop!

PIVOT STEP

No opponent will want to let you make a pass or take a shot on the basket after that rapid dash and sudden stop. But first you have to look: where are my teammates and how can I get off a successful shot on the basket? For that you need some time and space, but now you are not allowed to continue running with the ball or dribbling it. Now you need the pivot step!

The jump stop allows you to choose your supporting leg and your playing leg. When doing the one-two step stop, the leg that comes down first is always your supporting leg.

The **playing leg** is allowed to move.

The **supporting leg** is allowed to pivot but must remain in place.

PROTECTING THE BALL

As soon as you have the ball your opponents will of course try to take it away from you. They want to prevent you from taking a successful shot on the basket or passing the ball to a teammate. That is why you have to hold on tightly to the ball and protect it, so it can't be knocked out of your hand.

You watch the action closely.

The ball is held firmly with both hands.

The ball is held with the fingers and the thumbs point to the inside.

The feet are planted about shoulder width apart for a secure stance.

PASSING

A pass is always faster than dribbling. If no one is positioned between you and your teammate, you can pass the ball to him.

Success is more likely if you play together.

Chest pass

The chest pass is the most basic pass that all other passing variations are based on. If you can execute it well and reliably you will also be able to successfully perform the other techniques.

This is how the chest pass is executed:

- *You stand in the basic position with your legs slightly astride.*

- *Hold the ball to the side.*

- *The thumbs point up.*

- *For a straight motion the elbows stay close to the body.*

Make sure that the pass to your teammate is on target. It should be fast enough so no opposing player can intercept it. But it also shouldn't be too hard or your teammate won't be able to catch it.

- *The ball is passed by extending the arms in the direction of the pass and pushing from the wrists and fingers.*
- *At the same time the palms are rotated out.*

- *As the ball leaves the hands the arms are extended and the wrists are bent down.*
- *The torso moves forward slightly in passing direction.*
- *Always keep your balance!*

You can also pass like this

Depending on the game situation, you can opt for different kinds of passes. Once you have practiced different variations you can choose the best one.

Don't take chances! Always make a pass the safest way you can.

Overhead pass

If the opponent is pressuring you and you want to play over him, pass the ball high to your teammate.

- *The ball is held overhead with both hands and the thumbs nearly touch.*

- *The elbows are bent and point forward.*

- *The arms are forcefully extended forward whereby the hands remain overhead.*

- *To make the pass the hands are forcefully thrust forward.*

Pass with floor contact

You can make a bounce pass with one or both hands. The ball is bounced off the floor so it reaches the teammate when it bounces back up.

$^2/_3$

$^1/_3$

To the receiver.

One-handed pass

For this pass you play the ball like a handball player. That is why it is sometimes also called a handball pass. If you want to span a greater distance, throw the ball at head level or above.

One-handed passes are also used to make a lateral pass past an opponent to a teammate.

Try to play many different passes with one hand.

MISTAKES YOU SHOULD AVOID WHEN PASSING

Take a look at the way these players are passing. What are they doing wrong?

3

4

5

You will find the answers on the solutions page!

RECEIVING

The offensive players want to pass the ball back and forth until one player gets an opportunity for a shot on the basket. If they lose the ball the opposing team can mount its own offensive and score points.

This is how you receive the ball:

- *The players stands in the basic position.*
- *The hands are ready to catch and are extended in direction of the ball.*
- *The fingers are slightly spread and the thumbs point toward the body.*
- *The arms are pointed toward the ball and the elbows are slightly bent.*
- *The feet are positioned slightly astride and the weight is on the ball of the foot.*

- The ball is received with both hands with the fingers slightly spread.

Catch the ball with your fingers and don't let it "slap" your palms!

The ball is passed to the teammate from the chest and it is caught the same way – at the chest.

After you catch the ball you can dribble, pass it on or do the pivot step before you pass.

- *You accept the ball as though you were sucking it to your body.*
- *Draw the ball to your body.*
- *Slightly bend over the ball so the opponent can't knock it out of your hand.*

This is what you have to pay attention to when receiving the ball

The hands

- *The fingers are slightly spread.*
- *The hands close together so the ball cannot slip through.*

When catching the ball the hands form a **funnel** and the thumbs point to each other.

With a little imagination you can see a **W** or a **triangle** being shaped by your splayed fingers and thumbs when you look at your hands.

The arms

- *The arms are just slightly extended and reach toward the incoming ball.*

- *The impact of the ball is absorbed during the catch. To do so you pull your arms toward your body.*

- *The ball must be held securely to protect it from the opponent.*

You can easily catch and cushion against the impact of the ball with those "elastic" fingers, hands and arms. If you hear a slapping sound, something went wrong.

The legs

- *The ball is received in the basic position or stride position.*

- *The legs are shoulder-width apart and the knees are slightly bent. This gives you a firm stance so a hard pass won't knock you down.*

If a pass comes in farther to the side than expected, you can make a quick lunge to the side. This would allow you to also catch balls like that.

MISTAKES YOU SHOULD AVOID WHEN RECEIVING THE BALL

Take a look at the way these players are catching. What are they doing wrong?

A basketball player must be able to catch well. Poor and incorrect receiving can result in injuries to hands and fingers. And besides, your team loses the ball and with that a chance to make a shot at the basket.

HOW YOU CAN PRACTICE PASSING AND CATCHING

With good team play you can quickly move down the court. The best-positioned player gets the ball and attempts a shot at the basket. For that an accurate pass with the right amount of hardness and a solid catch are very important.

1 Pushing against the wall

Hold the ball with both hands in front of your chest. Push the ball from in front of your body against the wall. The hands always stay on the ball.

- *Start a short distance from the wall.*
- *Gradually increase the distance to the wall.*

2 Passing against the wall

Pass the ball against the wall, let it bounce once on the floor and then catch it.

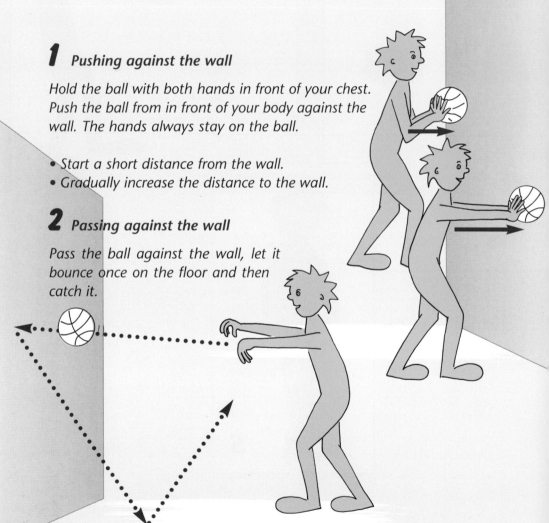

You can use a wall if you want to practice by yourself. But make sure the wall is suitable and you are not disturbing anyone!

3 Passing and receiving with a partner

Of course having a partner is great! You can practice passing and receiving at the same time. Keep playing the ball back and forth!

- *Pass the ball so your partner can receive it easily.*
- *Pass it so your partner cannot receive it easily.*
- *Pass it sometimes at knee level, at chest level or overhead.*
- *To the right and to the left.*
- *Sometimes a gentle toss, sometimes a hard throw.*
- *Slow and fast.*
- *Clap your hands before catching the ball.*

How many passes can you make in 10 / 15 seconds?

4 *Passing and receiving with several players*

Passing and receiving is really fun when there are several people to practice with.

- *Stand in a circle and keep passing the ball clockwise.*
- *Mix it up so no one knows whom the pass will go to.*
- *Play with two balls instead of just one.*
- *Each player starts with ten points. If he can't catch the ball he loses a point. Who is the last one to lose his points?*

Once you have tried an exercise, color in the ball!

SHOOTING AT THE BASKET

There are many ways of shooting a basket. Most important for the player is that the ball goes in the basket.

There are different shooting techniques a player should learn and master. Then he can react correctly in any situation.

Standing throw

- *The throwing hand is behind the ball and the other hand supports the ball from the side.*
- *The wrist of the throwing hand is tilted back.*

- *The elbows point to the basket.*

- *In the basic position the body's center of gravity is countersunk by the bending of the knees.*

- *The feet are parallel and the weight is distributed between both legs.*

- *You can also assume a slight stride position. (Right hand throws – right foot forward!)*

For the actual shot the throwing arm is extended upward.

As it releases the ball the throwing hand loosely folds down.

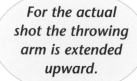

To make the shot the body straightens up ...

... and the legs are extended.

If you can't make it to the basket you can also hold the ball in front of your chest in the basic position.

Lay-up

The lay-up guarantees a successful completion most of the time because it occurs so close to the basket. You can dribble up to the basket and take a shot with a one-legged jump to the basket. But it is also difficult because the step sequence must be executed without mistakes.

If you bend your knees before the jump you will have even more momentum.

This is how the lay-up is executed

Begin by dribbling once about six yards from the basket.

- *The rhythm is as follows:
Right – left – jump with the right leg
or left – right – jump with the left leg.*

- *You dribble once and at the same time move towards the basket.*

- *After the jump you take the ball in both hands and bring it up towards the basket.*

- *The outside leg generates the momentum and the knee comes up.*

MISTAKES YOU SHOULD AVOID
WHEN DOING A LAY-UP

Take a look at the way these players are doing a lay-up. What are they doing wrong?

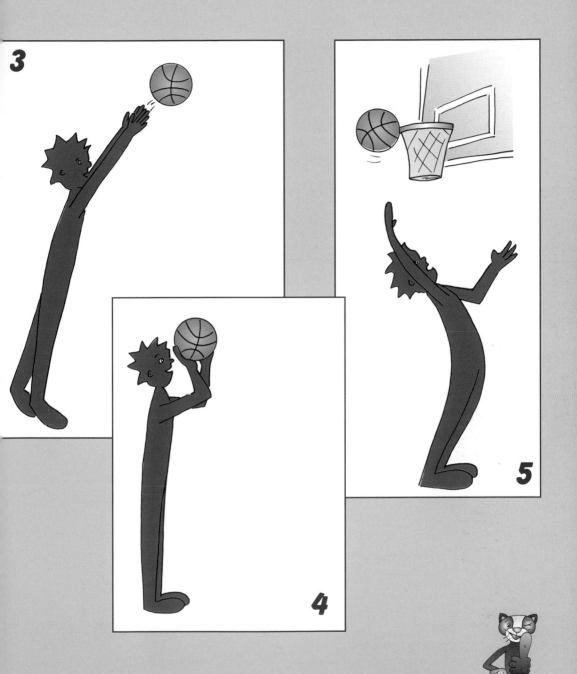

A good execution of the technique increases the chances for a successful shot.

THIS IS HOW YOU CAN PRACTICE THE LAY-UP

If you find yourself in a good shooting position you want to be able to score the points. To be able to shoot reliably you have to know the proper execution of the technique and practice lots and lots!

- *Throw the ball against the wall so it doesn't touch the wall until it starts to drop down (like the orange line shows)!*

1 Throwing against the wall

Look for a suitable wall and hold the ball with both hands in front of your chest like you do when you make a pass. Now pass the ball from in front of your body against the wall.

2 From the backboard to the basket

Use the backboard as an aid and throw the ball into the basket via the backboard. Aim for the upper corner of the square behind the basket.

3 Shooting a basket from different positions

Except for a free throw the player rarely has the opportunity during a game to leisurely pick the best distance in front of the basket and take a shot.

That is why you have to practice shooting baskets from different distances. Keep changing your position relative to the basket.

4 Shooting baskets without a basket

There aren't many opportunities to practice with baskets in a gym outside of the regularly scheduled training sessions. Also not all young basketball players have access to a basketball hoop at home. But that's not a problem! There are other options. Shoot over a tree branch, through a tire hanging from a tree, etc. Surely you and your friends can come up with some good ideas!

Make sure the ball can't roll too far away or you will just be busy chasing after it!

97

REBOUNDS

Not every shot goes in the basket. After a missed shot where the ball bounces off the backboard or the hoop, the players from both teams try to secure the ball.

Boxing out

When an offensive player takes a shot on the basket the defenders of course hope he will miss. They are prepared for a missed shot, are instantly ready to fight for the ball and start their own attack.

The defensive players keep their eyes on the opponents and position themselves between their offensive player and the basket. If you can see that your opponent wants to fight for the rebound you try to box him out by not letting him get to the ball (as the picture shows).

Be careful! No fouling! Stick to the rules when boxing out! Holding is not allowed!

Whoever jumps at the right moment and can jump the highest has the best chance of securing the rebound.

Securing the ball

Once you have your opponent under control you have to focus on securing the ball.

- *Watch the ball and jump so you can catch the ball at the highest point of your jump.*

- *Once you have the ball in your hands, pull it to your chest to secure it.*

- *Hold on tight to the ball so an opponent won't knock it out of your hands.*

- *Squeeze the ball with both hands and let your elbows stick out to the side a little.*

99

. . . . . . *8 PLAYING AS A TEAM*

You can shoot hoops by yourself or practice with your friends. But it's really fun when you turn it into a competition. Who gets the most baskets; who can intercept a pass or prevent a basket?

Basketball is actually a team sport. All the players on a team fight together to win. That is what's so special and nice about this sport.

Every basketball player plays as well as he can and does his best for the team, regardless of whether the team consists of five players or less. Every player has a job to do in defense or offense.

In order for team play to be successful every player has to adhere to a common plan – the team tactics!

101

OFFENSE

The offensive players try to keep the ball in their ranks by passing it until one of the players gets in a good shooting position. Once a player has reached a good position he takes a shot at the basket.

Anyone who doesn't have the ball gets open and makes himself available. Use eye contact and hand signals to show your teammates that you are ready for the ball.

OFFENSIVE ACTIONS

Forward player with the ball

From the basic position the forward player can
- shoot at the basket
- pass to a teammate
- dribble to a better position

Since the opposing defense won't just stand there and watch, the forward player must get past the defense. He can do this through
- deception
- cutting
- working with teammates

Forward player without the ball

The forward player without the ball
- keeps his eyes on the opposing defense
- gets himself open
- offers himself to receive the pass.

The opposing defense will not want to allow this either. That is why the forward player without the ball must trick them with skillful moves and deceptions.

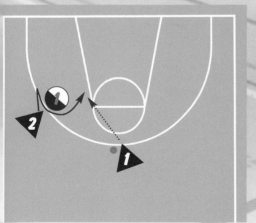

Example "Give and Go"

Two forward players play together. Forward number 2 fakes a cut to the left toward the basket and then suddenly cuts to the right, just past the defender, to the basket.

Forward number 1 passes him the ball. Forward number 2 can then finish the play with a lay-up.

DEFENSE

Once a team has scored a basket or lost the ball, all players must run to the other half of the court. The opposing players will attempt to score a basket with a fast break. Every defender should contain his opponent by the time they reach the center line. That includes always being on an imaginary line between the opponent and the basket. Move with quick sliding sideways steps. Always keep your balance.

We play **man-to-man defense**. That means every defender plays against one offensive player.

104

DEFENSIVE ACTIONS

Defense against the forward player with the ball

If your opponent has the ball and has not yet dribbled, you should keep some distance so you are able to react. You put pressure on him:

- force him to dribble
- force the dribbler to the outside
- try to make him stop and pick up the ball
- try to hinder his attempt to pass the ball

Defense against the forward player without the ball

If your opponent does not have the ball, you have to make it difficult or even impossible for him to receive a pass. At the same time you keep an eye on the action and the ball.

- If the ball is farther away you can fall back a little toward the basket.
- If the ball is so close that a short pass could reach your opponent, you hold your hand (thumb down) in the line between the player in possession of the ball and your opponent.

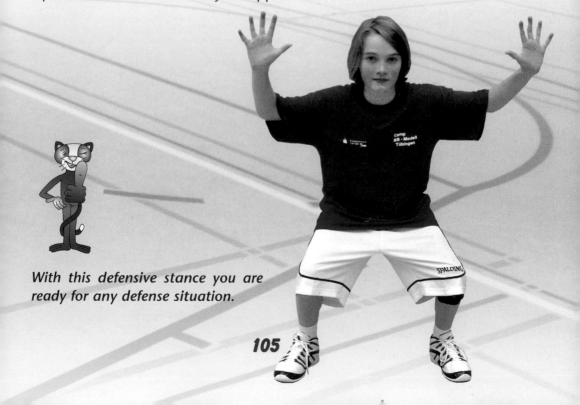

With this defensive stance you are ready for any defense situation.

105

Every game begins with a jump ball.

But our players and the referee look pretty bland. Not a problem: you can color them in!

106

· · · · · · · · · · · · · · *9 KEEPING THINGS STRAIGHT*

Almost everything in people's lives is regulated. What a mess it would be if everyone could just do whatever they wanted. Each family has rules that everyone has to abide by. Schools, day care, and sports teams do, too. There are traffic rules for road traffic, and every card game has rules.

It is the same in sports. Every sport has rules on how the sport is practiced, how a competition proceeds, and when a team wins or loses. There are also regulations for what is allowed and what is prohibited.

In basketball there is an entire book of rules. Thank goodness it is like that! Otherwise there would be a lengthy discussion about actions, baskets and penalties after every play and no one would enjoy the game. But we don't want to write about all of the basketball rules here. That would be too much and not that important for you right now. When you play with friends you can make your own rules, and at the club the coaches will explain anything that's important.

If you are interested you can read the official basketball rules on-line at www.nba.com. Please note that different leagues can also have different rules and that changes are occasionally made. This also applies to the rules in mini-basketball, which we will elaborate on in the second volume.

THE MOST IMPORTANT OFFICIAL RULES

Anyone who enjoys playing basketball can easily find a suitable place to play in a gym, on the street, in the park or on a playground. Boundaries and lines aren't that important. Together you can discuss and determine the number of players and the playing time.

But every basketball player should also be familiar with the most important official rules.

The court

- An official **NBA basketball court** measures 94 feet by 50 feet.
- An important marker is the **3-point line**. Every basket scored from outside of this large semi-circle counts three points.
- Baskets scored from inside the 3-point line count two points.
- After a foul a free throw is executed from the free throw line. A successful free throw counts one point.

Court length 94 feet

3-point line

23 feet 9 inches

Free throw line

13 feet

Base line 12 feet

Court width 50 feet

The team

Every basketball team has five players on the court.

The basket

- A court has two baskets.
- They are mounted at a height of 10 feet.
- They have a diameter of 18 inches.

Basket diameter 18 inches

Basket height 10 feet

Game start

Every basketball game begins with a jump shot at the center circle. The players try to tip the ball to their teammates with a high jump.

Playing time

- NBA basketball games are played in four 12-minute periods. NCAA games are played in two 20-minute halves. International games are played in four 10-minute periods.
- If the game is tied at the end of regulation time the game goes into 5-minute overtime periods until one team emerges the winner.

Time regulations

- The offensive team must take a shot on the basket within 24 seconds (shot clock).
- A player can hold the ball no longer than 5 seconds.
- The ball must be moved into the opposing court half within 8 seconds (back court violation).

Out-of-bounds ball

- A ball is out-of-bounds if it touches the floor, a wall, an object or a person on or outside of the boundary lines.
- If a team causes an out-of-bounds ball the opposing team is awarded a throw-in.

Traveling

Whenever a player wants to move forward with the ball he has to observe the following restrictions:

- When a player catches the ball during a jump he may take only one step per foot to shoot or pass the ball or to stop.
- When a player catches the ball while standing he may pivot around the supporting foot.
- When a player begins to dribble the ball must have left the hand before the supporting foot can leave the floor.

A traveling error is punished with a throw-in for the opposing team.

Fouls

- A personal foul refers to a player foul with direct contact with the opponent (i.e. holding, pushing, jostling).
- If the shooter is fouled he gets two free throws, or three free throws if the shot was taken from outside the 3-point line.
- If the basket was good in spite of the foul, the basket counts and the shooter gets an additional free throw.
- A foul on a player who is not involved in a shooting action results in a throw in for that player's team.

Dribbling

While dribbling the player may not:

- dribble with both hands at the same time.
- let the ball rest in one or both hands and then resume dribbling.

When the referee calls a foul the player in question lifts his arm to admit to the foul. This is a special sign of fairness in basketball.

FAIRNESS COMES FIRST

⬤ Be fair to your opponent

It is impossible to play basketball properly without athletic opponents. Or do you want to shoot baskets by yourself all the time? Therefore you should always show consideration and fairness to your opponents.

⬤ Be fair to your teammates

Everyone does his best and no one makes mistakes deliberately. Yelling and insults don't help anyone. It is better to help the weaker player so he will soon be able to support the team, because you can only be successful as a team.

⬤ Be honest

Be honest with yourself! Whenever you can't get to a ball, play it out of bounds or something doesn't go the way you would like, don't blame others but look to yourself first for the mistake. Play by the rules even when the referee isn't looking!

HEY, WHY DON'T YOU GUYS WANT TO PLAY WITH ME ANYMORE?

Playing, practicing and preparing for a game together and fighting for victory with the team – that's the greatest! You learn to value friendship, cooperativeness and camaraderie. Athletes conduct themselves fairly!

111

THE LITTLE MEN ARE VIOLATING THE RULES

Take a look at the way these players are playing. Can you tell which rules they are violating?

Do you know any other rule violations? List them here!

_____

_____

_____

THE REFEREE

At an actual competitive game where baskets, victory and defeat are at stake, it is important to have at least one referee umpire.

- He umpires the game and makes sure that the rules are adhered to.
- He directs the game so everyone enjoys playing.
- He will try very hard not to show favoritism towards either team.

The referee is in charge and all of the players must accept his calls. That also applies when you may have seen the situation differently and would make a different call.

REFEREE HAND SIGNALS

Basketball games in a gym are very noisy. The spectators cheer their team and the players call to each other. At international competitions the players of both teams and the referee often speak different languages.

To make sure that all of the players have a clear understanding of the referee's calls and to avoid misunderstandings, universal hand signals are used. That also makes it easier for you as a spectator in the gym or in front of the television to follow the referee's calls.

You can see some of the most important referee signals and their meaning on the adjacent page.

1 Jump ball

2 2-point shot

3 3-point shot

4 Traveling

5 Illegal dribbling

6 Foul

10 READY FOR THE BADGE?

The German Basketball Federation has a great concept! All children who enjoy playing basketball can earn a player badge.

Basketball players as well as teachers and coaches receive their information from the German Basketball Federation (DBB).

Maybe you would like to introduce a similar program at your club or school. You can adopt the requirements from the following pages or adapt them to suit your organization.

Who can acquire the player badge?

All children and adolescents who enjoy and are interested in basketball.

• Recreational players
• Student athletes
• Club players

Where can you acquire the player badge?

• At school
• At a club
• In a sports group
• At a basketball class

How does it work?

To earn the player badge there are specific tasks the young players need to fulfill. Your teachers or coaches will tell you what those tasks are.

YOU WANT TO KNOW HOW YOU CAN EARN THE PLAYER BADGE? HERE ARE THE REQUIREMENTS.

BADGE

Basketball

General information

The basketball player badge is issued by the **German Basketball Federation**. It represents an award for proficient abilities in recreational and popular sports. The basketball player badge is awarded in three levels. The **bronze badge** can be earned within the scope of a basketball meeting or the first practice session of a basketball class.

The **silver player badge** can be earned after completion of a 6 to 8 hour basketball clinic or instruction at school or at a club.

The **gold player badge** can be earned after a 6-month basketball course at school or at a club.

The badge requirements are the same for all age groups. Anyone can earn a basketball player badge. It is not necessary to be a member of a club. Each athlete receives a record book and a pin after passing the player badge test.

Process

Anyone who intends to acquire the player badge should participate in the events offered by clubs and schools, such as basketball meetings, a trial lesson or practice sessions. Taking the player badge test is free. Tests are administered at schools by teachers and at basketball clubs. Any organized or non-organized athletic organization as well as all schools and sports groups can order the necessary basketball player badge materials (record books and pins) from the German Basketball Federation business office for a small processing fee.

BADGE

Basketball

Bronze

Passing & Receiving Standing position: 10 successful passes with a partner. More than 10 attempts can be made. Distance between partners is approx. 11 feet.

Dribbling for a distance of approx. 10 yards. Forward movement by dribbling only, preferably one-handed. Dribbling should be done with the right hand in one direction and back with the left hand. Interruption of dribbling by catching the ball is permitted. If the ball rolls away it can be retrieved. Dribbling resumes at the place where the ball was lost.

Standing throw 6 shots: minimum of 4 shots must make contact with the hoop or 1 successful basket. Distance to the hoop is approx. 7 feet.

Game Participation in a basketball game with largely simplified rules. Game duration at least 5 minutes; play with one or two baskets, depending on team size (at least 3 players per team) and spatial availability; facilitation of team play through methods such as creation of specific passing stations and superior number situations.

Test successfully completed

....

Signature of examiner

....

Place and date

BADGE

Basketball

Silver

Passing & Receiving While moving: 3 fixed passing stations (one per "basketball circle" on the court. One pass back and forth without losing the ball with subsequent shot at basket (the shot at basket will not be scored).

Dribbling Slalom dribbling through 5 poles alternating hands (poles are approx. 9 feet apart), dribbling a distance of at least 30 yards in both directions without losing the ball with a subsequent shot on basket (shot on basket will not be scored). Ball cannot be held.

Standing throw 10 shots, at least 3 successful baskets. Distance to the hoop approx. 10 feet.

Lay-up 10 shots with the "strong hand"; at least 4 successful shots; jump-off from one leg, "wrong leg" permissible; choice of leg.

Game 2 x 10 minutes consecutive playing time with simplified rules; 5-minute breaks between halves. No player substitutions; up to 7 players per team.

Test successfully completed

....
Signature of examiner   *Place and date*

BADGE

Basketball

Gold

Passing & Receiving regulation passing and receiving while moving; passing back and forth from basket to basket and back without losing the ball with subsequent shot at the basket (shot at the basket will not be scored)

Dribbling Slalom dribbling around 5 poles alternating hands (distance between poles approx. 8 feet); 3 passes in both directions without losing the ball with subsequent shot on basket (shot on basket will not be scored). Execution criteria: regulation, covering the ball, looking up.

Standing throw 20 shots from the free throw line; at least 3 successful baskets, or 10 shots from a distance of 10 feet with 7 successful baskets.

Lay-up 10 shots with the "strong hand", each after dribbling from basket to basket (or around a marker at the center line); at least 7 successful baskets.

Game 2 x 15 minutes consecutive playing time with simplified rules; 5-minute break between halves. Each team consists of 5 players. No player substitutions.

Test successfully completed

....
Signature of examiner   *Place and date*

THE BASKETBALL QUIZ

We have listed four possible answers to each question. But only one of these is the correct answer. Can you find it?

 What is another name for a basketball player?

A	Ball thrower	B	Hoopster
C	Jumper	D	Basket collector

② What is another word for the ball bouncing off the backboard?

A	Dropper	B	Bouncer
C	Banger	D	Rebound

③ Where else is basketball played outside of the gym?

A	On sand	B	In the forest
C	On ice	D	On the moon

④ What is a "lay-up"?

A	A serious foul	B	The basket is falling down
C	A basket	D	A defeat

. . . . 11 LET'S PLAY!

To you the best game is of course basketball. And you want to play as much as possible.

But sometimes there aren't enough players, there are too many kids, you want to play in the schoolyard without markers, and there aren't any baskets either. Or you just want to bring a little variety to the game.

The following pages offer game ideas for all occasions. And along the way you practice the actual basketball techniques: receiving, passing, dribbling, shooting, etc.

You're it!

2 players

Both children are dribbling a ball. One child tries to tag the other with his free hand. Once he succeeds they switch roles.

Stay – Go

Many players

All of the players have a ball and dribble down the playing area. There is a catcher who tries to tag the other players. Anyone who gets tagged has to stop. He can only be released with a touch from another player.

Switching sides

Many players

All of the players have a ball and are lined up along a line. A short distance away on the opposite side at another line stands the catcher with a ball. He calls out, "Who is afraid of me?" All of the children shout, "No one!" and try to dribble their ball -with the right or left hand- as quickly as possible past the catcher to the opposite side. He of course tries to catch one of the children to help him during the next pass. Who is best at dodging the catchers? He will be the next catcher.

Bumper cars

Many players

All of the players dribble in a small area.

Rule 1:   No one can touch another player.
Rule 2:   The players try to knock each other's ball away.

Shadow dribbling

2 players

Two players stand one in front of the other and dribble their ball. One dribbles the ball in various ways and the other one tries to copy him like a shadow. You can also add some funny additional movements: taking off a jacket, scratching your head, singing, etc. You'll have lots of fun with it!

Mirror image dribbling

2 players

Two players stand facing each other while dribbling their ball. One dribbles in various ways and the other one tries to imitate him like a mirror image.

This game is also very fun but a little more difficult than the shadow dribbling.

Partisan ball

2 teams

Two teams are formed and move within an area marked with boundaries. The players on one team play the ball to each other. The players on the other team try to intercept the ball. If they are successful they will play the ball to each other and try to keep it in their ranks for as long as possible. Count the passes.

Variation 1:   The team that accumulates 10 passes gets a point.
Variation 2:   Which team will set the record – the most passes in a row?

Surely you can think of even more games with a basketball. Try changing the rules or come up with some games of your own. Have fun!

HELP, I'M LOST!

Picture this! At the last tournament I was in another city at an unfamiliar stadium. I had to make a quick trip to the restroom. But afterwards I couldn't find my way back to the basketball court.

Can you figure out which way I needed to go?

RESTROOM

GYMNASIUM

.... 12 FIT AND HEALTHY

Most people who play sports want to have fun and succeed. But an additional important goal is keeping one's body fit and healthy. Athletes therefore try to maintain a healthy lifestyle.

EATING RIGHT

Someone who participates in sports, runs and jumps, uses up more energy than a couch potato. That is why food always tastes best after those practice sessions – because you are hungry and thirsty and have to replenish your energy supply.

Almost all children like to eat hamburgers, chips, French fries, and pizza. But that's not the best food for athletes, particularly if you eat these things too frequently and in large quantities. These foods contain too much fat.

The better meal for an athlete consists of whole grain bread with cheese, pasta, fruit and yoghurt. There are many foods that are healthy and taste good, too. Try to have a varied and moderate diet.

This athlete is really hungry after practice. He would like to just eat and drink everything at once. What would you recommend? Cross out anything that in your opinion is not very healthy!

Which food should you eat more frequently during the day, and when you need a snack? Cross out every L, Y, M, A, X, E, K and D and read the word!

F	D	K	A	R	E	X	Y	M	L	A
M	E	L	M	A	U	D	I	K	D	Y
Y	A	D	D	L	K	Y	M	A	M	T

IF YOU SWEAT YOU HAVE TO DRINK REGULARLY

When you sweat during training and while playing, your gym clothes are often soaked and you can see beads of perspiration on your skin. Sweating isn't bad – in fact, it's very healthy. But your body misses the fluids you lose when you sweat. That's when you have to drink a lot so your body once again has enough fluids.

Your trainer, coach or teacher will plan water breaks when you have been sweating.

Don't choose drinks that are really cold or your body has to expend additional energy to warm up that fluid and get it up to body temperature!

Thirst quenchers

The best thirst quenchers are:

• Water, uncarbonated mineral water
• Water and juice mix (apple, orange or cherry juice mixed with water).
• Herbal tea or fruit tea (also sweetened with honey).

Pure juice and soft drinks are not suitable for replenishing fluids. They contain too much sugar.

When you are thirsty and drink, you have to be careful not to drink too hastily. It is better to take smaller sips more often. Be careful not to fill your stomach so full that you will barely be able to move.

DON'T FORGET TO WARM UP!

Surely your coach always does a warm-up at the beginning of a training session.

It is important that your muscles become warm, loose and flexible through different exercises. That is how you protect yourself from injuries.

To warm up you can jog or do some easy jumping exercises.

Swing your arms or move them in circles.

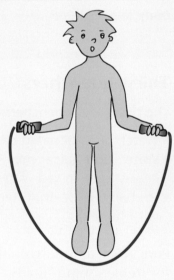

Dribble the ball at a walk and at a run. As you dribble, jump, spin around and clap your hands.

Even when you do exercises at home or play with your friends – don't forget to warm up!

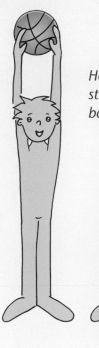

Holding the ball overhead, stretch yourself really long and stand on your toes – like you are trying to lay the ball in the basket.

Now bend over with straight legs and set the ball down.

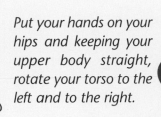

Put your hands on your hips and keeping your upper body straight, rotate your torso to the left and to the right.

Lie flat on your back and lift your pelvis off the floor.

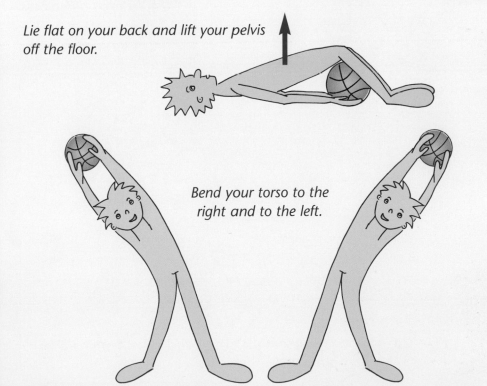

Bend your torso to the right and to the left.

A basketball player has to be very observant and must be able to assess any situation during a game. How observant are you?

Find eleven differences between the two drawings!

. . . . 13 PLAYING FOR A CLUB

At some point you realize that playing in the backyard, on the playground or at the park just isn't enough anymore. That's when it's time to join a club! There you can play on a team, be part of the action and play in real competitions.

HOW DO YOU FIND A CLUB?

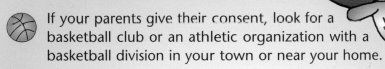 If your parents give their consent, look for a basketball club or an athletic organization with a basketball division in your town or near your home.

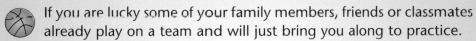 If you are lucky some of your family members, friends or classmates already play on a team and will just bring you along to practice.

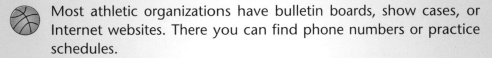 Most athletic organizations have bulletin boards, show cases, or Internet websites. There you can find phone numbers or practice schedules.

Make an appointment for tryouts. Bring your gear and take some time to watch how things work. You meet coaches and other children and see how the training is done. Of course everything will be new and strange at first. But that's normal.

Most of the time you will be asked how old you are and which age group you belong to. In a club placement on a team is done based on this information. It depends on the year you were born and not your school grade.

If you like it and the coach says that you are well suited for playing basketball, you should sign up. You will become a member of the club and receive a membership card.

MY FIRST BASKETBALL CLUB

This is where I play basketball:

_____

_____

My first day was on: _____

My coaches' names are: _____

Here you can paste a photo of your friends or a team picture.

MY FRIENDS AND TEAMMATES

On this page you can collect autographs from all of your friends in your training group.

GAME SCORES

Writing down the game scores is interesting and fun.

You can record them on these pages!

Opponent/Date	Score

Opponent / Date	Score

TO KEEP IT FUN FOR EVERYONE

First we want to tell you about a strange group of basketball players. Do you see what's going on here?

What is going on here?

The coach has already started the warm up when Tina comes running in with her boots on to get the key to the locker room. Tom can't jump properly because he is finishing his apple, Mia and Julie are having a loud conversation, Cory is crying because his jeans are to tight for pivoting, and Anne slipped in the apple juice Tammi spilled ...

Do you think practicing with this group is fun? Definitely not! Well, to be honest, we made this story up. It isn't really that bad anywhere. Or is there a little bit of truth to this story after all?

Rules are necessary

There are training rules to make sure that all children enjoy practicing and can learn well. These rules are established by the trainer or coach and are discussed as a group. All athletes make sure that the rules are adhered to. That way everyone can have fun practicing.

IMPORTANT RULES

Here is a list of rules we think are very important for the group and at the gym.

- ☺ Come to practice regularly and on time! Someone who dawdles misses a lot!

- ☺ Call and let someone know if you are sick. If your absence is unexcused, no one will know if you will be back to practice soon and whether you'll be able to play in the tournament!

- ☺ No talking during instructions and drills, or you won't understand everything and end up making mistakes!

- ☺ Wear suitable clothing!

- ☺ Don't enter the gym with street shoes! Choose tennis shoes with light colored soles so you won't leave black skid marks on the floor!

- ☺ The hoop and net are not for swinging from nor should they be used as gymnastics equipment.

- ☺ No eating or chewing gum in the gym!

- ☺ No drink bottles standing around in the gym.

- ☺ Help each other and be considerate of each other!

- ☺ _____

- ☺ _____

- ☺ _____

Do you have any other rules? List them on the blank lines!

. . . . 14 SOLUTIONS

Pg. 10   **In the picture:** basketball, volleyball, handball, hockey, soccer, tennis, football, ping-pong

            Here is what else we thought of: baseball, rhythmic gymnastics, polo, water polo

Pg. 14   Score!

Pg. 51   All of the players had black fingers because that is where they made contact with the ball while playing. The palms stayed white. That's the way it should be!

Pg. 56   The player catches the ball thrown by number 1.

Pg. 60/61 **Good or not good?**
1. The player is looking around and not focusing on the game.
3. The player stands stiffly with his knees hyperextended. That makes him not agile enough to react quickly in the game.
4. The position of the player's arms is uneven.
5. The player cannot receive a pass with his arms crossed.
6. To catch the ball reliably your hands should be closer together.

            Player number 2 has a good basic stance.

Pg. 66/67 Dribbling mistakes

1 The eyes are on the ball. The player cannot see his teammates or his opponent.
2 The player is dribbling too high. The ball can easily be taken away from him.
3 The player is dribbling with both hands. That is not allowed!
4 While running fast he needs to dribble the ball farther out front.
5 The player isn't dribbling with his whole fingers but only with the fingertips.

Pg. 78/79 Passing mistakes

1 The eyes are on the ball. The player cannot pass accurately.
2 The hands don't fold down and the thumbs point up.
3 The player's body isn't moving in the direction of the pass but is leaning back.
4 The ball is held incorrectly. The hands are holding the ball from the front.
5 The feet are too close together.

Pg. 84/85 Receving mistakes

1 The player is not focusing on the game.
2 The hands are too far apart.
3 The hands are too low for this ball.
4 The arms are extended too far and the thumbs point up.
5 The legs are too straight and the feet aren't shoulder-width apart.

Pg. 94/95 Shooting mistakes

1 The player is holding the ball incorrectly.
2 The body should come up with the ball at a slight angle. This player is shooting too shallow. The position of the right arm is incorrect.
3 The thumbs point up and the hand does not fold down.
4 During the preparation phase the player's knees should be slightly bent. Are the feet shoulder-width apart?
5 This player is leaning back while he is shooting.

Pg. 112/113 Rule violations
    1 The ball cannot be kicked with the foot.
    2 Contact with the floor can only be made twice with the ball in hand.
    3 Jostling or pulling hair are personal fouls.
    4 Holding is also a foul.
    5 The referee cannot be insulted!

Pg. 122 Basketball quiz
    1 B – Hoopster
    2 D – Rebound
    3 A – On the sand
    4 C – A basket

Pg. 126

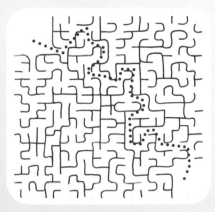

Pg. 128

F	D	K	A	R	E	X	Y	M	L	A
M	E	L	M	A	U	D	I	K	D	Y
Y	A	D	D	L	K	Y	M	A	M	T

Pg. 132

143

. . . . 15 LET'S TALK!

If this were a book for adults, these pages for the parents and trainers would of course appear at the very front of the book as the preface. But since it is a book for children we are putting this chapter at the end, sort of as an addendum.

Our beginning basketball players are mostly elementary school students who have not yet had very much exposure to books. They are absolutely in need of support from "big people" who can help them with the approach to the book. The best way to start is by leafing through the book, looking at the pictures and filling in and recording information. This book does not have to be read back to back, but can also be used as a reference work and a personal basketball diary.

Have fun reading together!

DEAR BASKETBALL PARENTS,

Do you remember the first time your little son or daughter chased after a ball and wanted to play with it? Surely you'll say: As soon as my child was able to walk! Your child never lost this fascination with the ball and has chosen one of the many ball sports. He or she wants to learn to play basketball, maybe even practice at a club with experienced coaches and well trained trainers. It is great that you want to support him or her in learning this appealing sport.

Basketball is a sport for boys as well as girls. Basketball can be played as early as pre-school age and motivating experiences, such as controlling the ball when dribbling and shooting the first baskets, already occur as soon as the first basic elements have been learned. Basketball distinguishes itself through its diversity of movements, is demanding in terms of technique, agility, general skillfulness, and endurance, and promotes concentration and quick decision-making. Your child is part of a social community and learns the specifics of team play as well as the importance of the individual player. He or she learns to persevere and to deal with success and failure at games. Personal responsibility must be learned, too. By and by the players take responsibility for the care and completeness of the equipment and pay attention to punctuality and regularity in training and competition. So be supportive as your child learns to play basketball, practices and trains.

For our little players the enjoyment of playing, the movement, the dribbling, passing and catching as well as shooting baskets in the various forms of play initially outweighs everything else. Of course this does require some basic technique, but that should not be the main focus just yet. The children should play, have fun, and in doing so develop their skills. That is also our intention with this book. Next to the explanations of necessary basic technique and basketball rules the children also learn a lot about the game of basketball in general. They have the opportunity to become actively involved in their favorite sport.

Be helpful, but with prudence!

Do not let your expectations for your child get too high! What matters most is the enjoyment of the sport and playing. Excessive ambition would only be harmful. Don't compare your child to others of the same age, because biological development, particularly at this age, can vary greatly. Just focus on your own child and praise his or her progress. Your child will thank you.

OH BOY, OH BOY!
I PROMISE I'LL NEVER MISS
A SHOT AGAIN!

Support from basketball parents

Parental support is in demand in basketball, too. Be it for the organization of training attire, rides to games or chaperoning at tournaments. Surely Mom or Dad, or even Grandma or Grandpa have to be available as partners for playing and practicing as well as putting up that long-desired basketball hoop.

When your child is part of a team, some of your weekends will be affected by the playing activities. If a game is scheduled for Saturday or Sunday, the family has breakfast by the alarm clock, the parents are chauffeurs for part of the team, and the siblings want to come along to cheer. Sunday dinner has to wait until the game is over, and visits to Grandma's are only planned for non-game days. But what's better than seeing your own eager little player be irrepressibly happy about shooting his first basket? Or how much trust and intimacy parents and children experience when a defeat or a missed shot requires comforting. Be glad that your child is getting regular exercise. Regardless of whether your child will become an internationally successful super-player or is "only" enjoying the game and the camaraderie.

And one more thing:

Savor the game and enjoy the actions of the little basketball players. Cheer the children on and enjoy their successful plays. However, children find their parents' shouting during a game irritating. The children need to make their own decisions, and technical suggestions as well as substitutions are the trainer's responsibility.

DEAR BASKETBALL TRAINER, TEACHER AND COACH

Surely you'll agree that it is a great feeling to see these little guys with their excited faces and expectant eyes. Now it is up to you to introduce them to basketball.

But all children are different. There are the tall ones and the short ones, self-confident ones and the timid ones, the diligent and the not so diligent, the talented and the less talented. Each child has his or her own little personality with individual qualifications and his or her own developmental history, with hopes and desires, with feelings and needs. They all have our regard in equal measure. Children want to be active, to move and have fun. Particularly in a group they are able to match themselves with their peers and spur each other on.

A beginning basketball player's most important role model is the coach, teacher or trainer. They watch everything very closely: How he talks to them, how he handles the ball and executes the movements. They also pay close attention to how well their trainer adheres to the rules and safety regulations.

The young player himself is the most important factor in the teaching and learning process. The child, no matter how young and how much of a beginner he maybe, is always subject to his own development and

148

never just the object of our influence. Therefore offer enough tips and opportunities for their own development. Foster and utilize your little beginning basketball player's independence. Take the path from directing to inspiring. The children don't have to and aren't supposed to, but they can and they may.

The value of this little book

The value of this little book will depend entirely on how you will integrate it into the instruction. It is written specifically for children who are beginning basketball players. But it can also be recommended to parents who wish to accompany their child on this path. The book focuses on the

What a children's basketball trainer should have:

INCENTIVE, PRAISE COMFORT AND ENCOURAGEMENT FOR EVERYONE.

TECHNICAL KNOWLEDGE AND ORGANIZATIONAL SKILLS.

SOLUTIONS TO THEIR PROBLEMS.

A HEART FOR CHILDREN.

A GOOD SELECTION OF DRILLS AND EXERCISES.

GOOD COMMUNICATION WITH PARENTS.

THE ABILITY TO CONVEY A SENSE OF PLEASURE AND ENJOYMENT IN THE SPORT.

KNOWLEDGE OF CHILDREN'S PHYSICAL PARTICULARITIES AND DEVELOPMENTAL STAGES.

SKILL IN DEALING WITH CHILDREN.

children's needs and is intended to help them also engage in basketball outside of the gym. The child acquires a fairly complete foundation for practicing via the book's illustrations and descriptions. He will be better able to follow your explanations and demonstrations. The young players can review at their leisure what they have learned, keep track of goals and learning progress, and receive suggestions for practicing at home and with other children. This develops the ability to act independently and accelerates the learning process.

An environment is created in which the children themselves, step by step, think about their practicing and learning, their movements, actions, and finally monitor and evaluate their behavior. They become a partner to the coach and trainer. We would like the children to enjoy coming to practice and go home with a sense of achievement. And of course that would make the practice sessions fun for the trainer as well.

The book and training

Tell the children that this book will be their personal companion as they learn to play basketball. Give them the logo of the club and take a photo to paste in the book. This will boost their attachment to you, to the team and the club.

Help the children to use this book properly. In the beginning, read some segments together and explain to the children how the photos and illustrations should be viewed and understood. Together with the little players make entries regarding goals, suggestions, etc. In doing so you create critical orientation guides for their understanding and independent practicing. With the aid of this book you can also assign homework for the next training session. The children read up on a topic and get to do a show-and-tell at the next session.

We wish you and your little protégées lots of fun and enjoyment, and of course athletic successes, too.

151

19.9.2012

PHOTO & ILLUSTRATION CREDITS

Cover design: Jens Vogelsang
Illustrations: Katrin Barth
Cover photo: Imago
Photos (inside): Katrin Barth, Lothar Boesing, DBB/Camera 4 (photo
                pg. 24, 27) German Basketball Federation, Celine
                Mayer, Bianca, Jürgen and Sandra Metze, Dirk Nowitzki